Written simply, clearly and humbly [...]
look up and see God's glory from th[...]
And then to be changed by the sight.

Andrew Cornes,
Former Minister, All Saints Crowborough

So often I have a small view of who God is and what He can do. In this little book Tom Robson encouraged me to use my imagination to have a bigger view. Thinking over these four vivid pictures of God's glory in the Bible gave me a glimpse of our eternal home in glory. That bigger view now is what will keep us going until we will see Jesus face to face.

Liz Cox,
Minister for Women & Community, St Giles' Church Derby and Chair of Midlands Women's Convention

Fresh and warmly written, Breathtaking Glory *unfolds a lovely view of the glory of God. In a few brief chapters Tom Robson shows us God's grace, faithfulness and ultimate triumph in Jesus Christ such that the reader is humbled, thrilled and edified in equal measure.*

Reuben Hunter,
Lead Pastor, Trinity West Church

BREATHTAKING
GLORY

BREATHTAKING
GLORY

SURVEYING THE PANORAMA OF
GOD'S GRACE, FAITHFULNESS AND VICTORY

TOM ROBSON

Copyright © 2020 by Tom Robson
First published in Great Britain in 2020

British Library Cataloguing in Publication Data
A record for this book is available from the British Library

ISBN: 978-1-912373-87-1

Designed and typeset by Pete Barnsley (CreativeHoot.com)

Photo by Daniel Leone on Unsplash
Printed in Denmark by Nørhaven

10Publishing, a division of 10ofthose.com
Unit C, Tomlinson Road, Leyland, PR25 2DY, England

Email: info@10ofthose.com
Website: www.10ofthose.com

1 3 5 7 10 8 6 4 2

DEDICATION

For Emily, Martha and Mollie

CONTENTS

INTRODUCTION

How would you react if I said you're destined for glory?

If you're a child prodigy, reading this in nursery whilst solving Fermat's last theorem with your ABC cubes, then it would come as no surprise. But for most of us, hopes of being destined for glory are probably long gone, or may never have arrived in the first place. If someone told me I was destined for glory, I think it would come across more sarcastic than supportive!

And yet, if you're trusting Jesus, you are heading towards a glorious destination. You are *destined* for glory – the glory of God, in whose presence will be greater joy than any of us can imagine.

Through the prophet Isaiah, God declared that he would bring his people to be with him. That promise was partly fulfilled at the time, but it also points forward to when all God's people will be gathered to glory: 'Bring my sons from afar and my daughters from the ends of the earth – everyone who is called by my name, whom *I created for my glory*' (Is. 43:6–7, my italics).

The New Testament develops the same promise. We are saved in order to be with God, to enjoy his glory forever. The apostle Paul, whilst discussing Jesus coming again, describes this gathering home of God's children: '[God] called you to this through our gospel, that you might *share in the glory* of our Lord Jesus Christ' (2 Thes. 2:14, my italics). Notice that Paul says we won't just see Christ's glory; we will share in it.

The hope of this gospel is that Christ can reset anyone on a path to share his glory; no one is too far off-track. Take the thief crucified next to Jesus. Here was a man seemingly destined for nothing but an agonising death. Yet his plea to Jesus is answered with the promise of a glorious destination: 'today you will be with me in paradise' (Luke 23:43).

We can all know the feeling that life isn't really heading anywhere. Maybe when you wonder about your future, you can't see how things will ever improve. If that's you, please listen to Jesus' promise. When we put our trust in Jesus, the best – by far – is still to come: 'our light and momentary troubles are achieving for us an eternal glory that far outweighs them all. So we fix our eyes not on what is seen, but on what is unseen, since what is seen is temporary, but what is unseen is eternal (2 Cor. 4:17–18).

But, if we fix our eyes on that glorious eternity, are we in danger of becoming 'so heavenly minded as to be of no earthly good?' as Oliver Wendell Holmes allegedly said. Actually, I'm convinced that the opposite is true. Anticipating your destination inspires the journey to get there. And the glory of our destination isn't really where it is or what it's like; it's the one with whom we'll be. The more we look forward to being with him, the more we will enjoy living for him on the way.

Imagine setting out on a long drive. I doubt anyone is motivated by the prospect of crawling through traffic jams and endless games of I Spy. Unless you're a big fan of ring roads, you'll set out because you have a destination in mind. When you're going to see someone special, even a difficult journey can be full of expectation.

Climbing a mountain is my favourite illustration of this. If you've ever walked, scrambled, or dragged yourself up a mountain, I hope it provided you with a glorious view. Yet, for most people, the way up is hard work. The paths are steep and uneven; there are unexpected twists and dangerous falls. So you proceed carefully, watching your footing. But no one climbs a mountain to stare at their feet; you're hoping for a panoramic reward when you reach the summit. And as you climb, you pause and catch your breath. You look up for a moment and take in an early sight of the landscape. Those glimpses whet your appetite for what's to come and motivate you to keep going. They're little previews that say, 'If you think this is good, wait until you get to the top!' I spend a lot of time watching my (metaphorical) footing. I try not to stumble through life's rocky patches and hope to stay on track. Unless you're gliding effortlessly through life, I imagine you might feel the same. When times are tough, it's only natural to focus on what's right in front of us.

We don't always make time to pause and take in the view, or remember the glory of where we're heading. Perhaps we're consumed by the busyness of life. Maybe we are rightly giving our time to people or situations we care about. Or possibly we're bruised from too many stumbles and now proceed cautiously – eyes down, one step in front of the other.

So in life, as on a mountain climb, it's good to catch your breath occasionally and look up. This book invites you to do that: to pause and take in an early view of the glory you're heading to in Christ. These are glimpses of God's glory that we'll one day enjoy in full. Here are the initial sights of the one whom we will enjoy forever. Indeed, the greatest motivation for trusting Jesus is not where we'll be, but the glory of the one with whom we'll be.

As we take in these sights of God's glory, I won't recommend too many things to do. I assume you have enough of those already. You might even be one of those people who has a to-do list of to-do lists you still need to write. Instead, I hope this is a chance to take a short break from those to-dos. Simply take in the glory of the God who made you, who died to save you and whose glory will fill you with joy now and forever.

GLORY

'Forever' is not an easy concept to get our heads around. The British politician Lord Mancroft once joked, 'Cricket is a game which the English, not being a spiritual people, have invented in order to give themselves some conception of eternity.'[1] But even five-day Test matches (eventually) come to an end. So how can an eternal destination inspire us if it's so hard to picture what it's like?

Then there's the feeling many people have that anything that lasts forever will eventually become boring. One of the deliberately infuriating characters in Joseph Heller's *Catch-22* is an airman called Dunbar. He sees this connection between longevity and boredom, and tries to extend his life by filling it with as much tedium as possible. When he's challenged on why he would want to experience a long life if it's so uninteresting, he simply replies, 'What else is there?'[2]

---

[1] Lord Mancroft, *Bees in Some Bonnets* (Bachman & Turner, 1979), p. 185.
[2] Joseph Heller, *Catch-22* (Vintage, 1994), p. 44.

The Bible's answer to both those questions is the same: eternity inspires us and promises limitless joy because we've seen what the Lord is like. When we fix our eyes on God's glory, we not only look forward to being with him forever but also know a foretaste of that joy in the here and now.

GLORY DEFINED

In general, there are two ways to use the concept of glory. The first relates to attributes of the world around us. We've already thought about the glory of a mountain-top view. Glorious in this sense describes something inherent in creation. It is the colours and landscapes that convey a beauty or magnificence, such as the glory that a sunset has simply by being a beautiful sunset.

The other way we think of glory is through victory or success. This second form of glory is one that is achieved. My closest brush with this type of glory came aged eleven on school sports day. In previous years my teams had never excelled in the competitive fields of bean-bag throwing and hoopla. But then, in my final year of primary school, I was given the honour of captaining one of the teams. Finally, it all came together; our elite band of sports stars triumphed through relay races, hopscotch and other high-precision events. We finished in first place and ran laps around the playground in celebration. As you can tell, it still ranks worryingly high on my list of life achievements. It must be the early tastes of glory that inspire future champions towards even greater success.

So when we find something glorious, it's because of its attributes or its achievements, but rarely both. A clear day following a heavy storm might be called a glorious morning, but it isn't praised for having created itself. On the other hand, a great artist might be called a glorious painter, but that is a result of the beauty she crafts on her canvas, not a glory in and of herself. Had she never picked up the brushes, she would never have received that praise. However, the characteristics both expressions of glory share is to be considered worthy of praise, honour and adulation. To be glorious is to have attributes or achievements that others enjoy celebrating.

To fully understand glory, we also need to recognise the impact it has on those who experience it, either for themselves or in someone else. It would be very odd to encounter something we find glorious and not be affected. Have you ever been at a performance that has been so moving you could describe it as glorious? There's something about glory that transcends the ordinary. In those moments we feel a desire to share the praise of it. We 'glory in it' and feel that others will lose out unless they do the same. It's like when a friend shows you photos of the 'glorious view' from their trip. They want you to share their amazement as they sit you down for the slideshow.

However, even the most impressive photo is nothing compared to seeing the view for yourself. When we come face to face with something glorious, it lifts our sights above the routine. It reminds us that there's more to celebrate than we sometimes remember. Those are moments when the world does its best to take your breath away.

God's glory has a similar impact, but on a far greater scale. The Creator is revealed as utterly glorious in attributes *and* achievements. Scripture pictures God's glory as an overwhelming brightness and an unchanging goodness. This inherent glory is then perfectly mirrored in all God's actions. Seeing the glory of what the Lord has done is a window onto the glory of who he is. And an experience of his glory has a profound effect.

GLORY REVEALED

The Old Testament describes several encounters with God's glory, and no one comes closer than Moses. Having been called to lead his people out of Egypt, it is Moses' experience of God's glory that defines the next stage of their journey. When the Lord speaks to him from the burning bush, he is warned to keep his distance in case the glory of God's holiness consumes him (Ex. 3:5). This proximity to God's glory has a powerful effect on Moses. When the time comes for him to lead God's people towards the promised land, he seeks the assurance of God's presence going with them. Moses even pleads with the Lord to 'show me your glory' (Ex. 33:18). God agrees, but on one condition. His glory is so intense that Moses has to hide in the rock cleft, shielded by God's hand, as his presence passes by. That is the closest Moses can come. Even then, Moses' face shines as he comes down the mountain.

Fire and light continue to be the expression of God's glorious presence. After saving his people from Egypt, the Lord leads them through the desert in a fiery pillar of cloud. When they camp at the bottom of Mount Sinai, 'the glory of the LORD looked like a consuming fire on top of the mountain' (Ex. 24:17).

God's glory also has a powerful effect on his people. They are comforted by its presence but devastated by its absence. Before the construction of the temple, God's presence is known to reside in the ark of the covenant. This is so significant that when the Philistines defeat Israel and capture the ark, the daughter-in-law of Eli the priest laments, 'The Glory has departed from Israel' (1 Sam. 4:22). Later, when Ezekiel prophesies God's judgment on the Israelites' wickedness, his vision portrays God's glory departing from the temple (Ezek. 10). There is no greater indictment on their corruption than the removal of God's glorious presence.

Encounters with God's glory begin again in the New Testament. In particular, the early Christians see this same glory in Jesus. The apostle John, in the famous introduction to his Gospel, writes, 'We have seen his *glory*, the *glory* of the one and only Son, who came from the Father, full of grace and truth' (John 1:14, my italics). Or we could climb another mountain with Peter, James and John who witness the brightness of God's glory in Jesus' transfiguration. So what about us? With God's glory no longer residing in a temple, and God's glory in Christ ascended to heaven, are we able to see this glory?

We believe that his presence dwells amongst us through his Holy Spirit. Jesus told his disciples that this would be better than him remaining. We're blessed with joy, peace, hope and many other spiritual gifts that pre-Pentecost believers would have prized. But, being honest, doesn't this feel a little less *glorious* than fiery pillars and burning bushes? Can we pose a similar question to Moses and ask God to 'show us his glory'?

I believe that, because of God's grace, we can. Like Moses, we can go where the Lord leads, reassured of his presence and trusting in his goodness. Knowing and experiencing that glory will fill us with a unique sense of joy and wonder. And those glimpses of glory can inspire the whole of life's adventure.

GLORY EXPERIENCED

The Bible unfolds a vivid account of God's character and actions. God speaks through his Word and reveals his glory to those with eyes to see and ears to hear. Sometimes, though, we can fall into the trap of reducing it to information about God. But the purpose of Scripture is so much more than that, because the Lord uses it to draw us into his ongoing story. There are moments when our imagination can show us what God is like. As Scripture recounts actual events with actual people in actual places, we can picture what it is like to encounter the glory of God in Jesus. God's created us with the ability to form these mental images, so let's employ that gift and allow Scripture to be a fully immersive experience.

However, we sometimes neglect the role of imagination in the Christian faith. Perhaps we worry that imagining means creating false images of God. That's an understandable concern. And yet our imagination is also how we visualise those things that do exist. If you think of someone you know, your imagination can bring them to mind. If you think back to your last holiday, hopefully you can close your eyes and picture the scene. (If you can't, it's time to book another one!) I think that's partly why C.S. Lewis' writing maintains such an appeal. Not only his fiction but his whole writing style engages imagination so that we can almost feel the glory of God.

The question is how do we use our gift of imagination? I know when I let my imagination roam free, it often creates narratives in which I get the glory. But what happens when we allow God's Word to inspire our imagination to see his glory?

Jesus was the master of employing our imagination. His parables conjure memorable images, like a camel squeezing through the eye of a needle or a man swiping about with a great plank in his eye. My favourite is the man sprinting down a dusty road to embrace his returning son. As I picture that father running with his arms flung out wide, I can see God's glory in the love he shows to the prodigal.

That's what I mean by the way Scripture can be immersive. We can experience that same kindness from God when we turn from sin and receive his gift of forgiveness. The hug may be less tactile, but the love is just as real. The story of God's grace becomes our story. The glory portrayed in Jesus' parable becomes a glory that we know for ourselves.

As we will see, the Bible unfolds a wonderful revelation of God. If it was just a list of descriptions and definitions, it wouldn't have the same effect. Thankfully, the Bible doesn't only tell but also *shows* us who God is. It provides viewpoints from which to take in the glory of the Lord that we can enjoy now and forever. As I've looked out from these I've seen a vivid, inspiring and breathtaking glory. I hope you find the same.

TAKE IN THE VIEW

As we go along, I hope you will see why I've selected the four vantage points in the following chapters. I trust that by pausing to savour what they reveal to us about God, the next stage of your journey will be that much more expectant. Then when the path gets rocky, you can remind yourself of the one who made you and who died to save you. These are glimpses of God's breathtaking glory that say, 'If you think this is good, wait until you get to the top!'

So why not pause for a moment?

Ask God to inspire your imagination.

Ask him to show you his glory.

2

HUMAN SIN AND ANIMAL SKIN

THE GLORY OF GOD'S GRACE

*The LORD God made garments of skin for
Adam and his wife and clothed them.*

(Gen. 3:21–23)

Our first viewpoint on God's glory is Genesis 3, immediately after the account of creation. I realise it may seem odd to begin exploring God's glory in Genesis, and to skip over the first two chapters. Isn't God's glory displayed in all he made? What of the size and scale of stars, planets and galaxies? How about the intricate detail of creatures great and small?

Clearly, the created universe is a wonderful display of God's glory. John Calvin called it 'the theatre' of God's glory with good reason.[3] Every astrological discovery

---

[3.] John Calvin, *Institutes of the Christian Religion*, Book 1, p. 8.

adds to our understanding of how 'The heavens declare the glory of God' (Ps. 19:1). But I've chosen the third chapter of Genesis in order to take in another aspect of God's glory: his grace.

At the same time, we need to begin with God's creation in order to appreciate his grace. Out of nothing, God made a universe which reflects his goodness and beauty. At the pinnacle of this creation, he gave humanity the highest calling of all – to be made in his image and to steward earth's diversity of life. Best of all, God created us that we might know him, and share in the love that unites Father, Son and Spirit. This closeness is pictured as God walking in the garden with Adam and Eve. It's a beautiful portrayal that sets in hideous contrast what follows – humanity's rejection of the God who gives us life.

INGLORIOUS REBELLION

You could call it rebellion; you could call it a disaster. The Bible calls it sin. Sin, at its heart, is a rejection of God. It's a foolish attempt to overturn the distinction of Creator and creation. So, as we consider God's response to our sin, we see that it's about more than breaking laws; it's also about relationship. In fact, we can concentrate so heavily on the expressions of sin (actions opposed to God's will), that we forget the root cause (hearts opposed to God).

Genesis 3 describes Adam and Eve in close relationship with God, enjoying him and his provision of the garden. But the serpent tempts them to grab at something more – a false promise of becoming like God if they eat from the forbidden tree. They both knowingly eat, then discover that it was God and not the serpent who had their best interests at heart. As a result of this disobedience, their relationship with God lies broken in pieces.

We see that relational focus again when God later gives the Law through Moses at Mount Sinai. The first three of the ten commandments stress relationship with the Lord in contrast to false gods and idols. In fact, the whole context for the commandments is God's goodness towards them: 'I am the LORD your God, who brought you out of Egypt, out of the land of slavery' (Ex. 20:2). This should tell us that the Law is given for our good, and to maintain our walk with the Lord. The more we understand the relation-destroying nature of sin, the more we'll see the glory of the grace that overcomes it.

So sins are not a list of fun things that God has decided he doesn't like. He's not a grumpy teacher banning toys from the playground because he's grown tired of hearing children play. The rules that God lays down are not arbitrary. They are instructions for how people made in God's image can remain in a right relationship with him. God calls us to obey because he cares for us; he wants us to stay within his love and holy presence.

We will all have experienced the pain of broken relationships, some more acutely than others. I'm sure you know how hard those wounds can be to heal, and the personal cost required to forgive. Probably the closest (although imperfect) analogy we have is of parent and child. When my children don't do what I ask, I find it frustrating, especially as the instructions are hopefully intended for their good. But were they ever to disown me, to break that relationship off, I can't even imagine how that would feel. Our rebellion against God is of an even higher order. It separates us from an essential, life-giving union.

That is what our first representatives discovered, and it is captured in the haunting question of Genesis 3:9 immediately after they have eaten from the tree. God asks Adam and Eve, 'Where are you?' An all-seeing God doesn't need to ask that question. God knows exactly where they are. But his question reveals that the relationship has broken down. They have cut themselves off from God. They are lost.

Then follows their punishment for breaking God's only restriction. Eve will suffer the pain and worries of childbirth. Adam will endure the curse of the ground and eventually death. The punishment is serious because turning your back on the God who made you is deadly serious. This is about more than taking a piece of fruit. This is the account of a heartbreaking rebellion against a holy God and his loving care.

The glory of God's grace shines against this backdrop of human disobedience, for the same reason that jewellers display diamonds against a dark cloth. Acts of kindness always stand out when they're offered to undeserving recipients.

A few years ago, I was invited to meet a couple called Bill and Mary. They told me the story of their son: he was attacked by a drunk man on a night out and died of his injuries. He was only in his early twenties and had done nothing to provoke his attacker. The perpetrator was identified, arrested and sentenced to prison for manslaughter. But, before he was released, Mary and Bill arranged to see him. Over several meetings, they got to know the man who killed their son and, incredibly, they forgave him. When he was released, they helped him find a job, and they are still supporting him today. For me they are a wonderful embodiment of grace – undeserved and costly love.

GRACIOUS PROVISION

God's grace is at work just two verses after Adam and Eve's sin as 'God made garments of skin for Adam and his wife and clothed them' (Gen. 3:21). Adam and Eve have become aware of their nakedness immediately after tasting the fruit. It is the initial indicator that it was the serpent who'd lied because they feel shame for the first time. Yet their nakedness is the very thing for which God provides. He clothes them, without a hint of 'I told you so.'

There's no doubt that the relationship between God and humanity drastically changes because of the Fall. From then on, sin becomes a barrier to the closeness and intimacy that was originally intended. But the consistent message from Genesis onwards is that God continues to love and provide for Adam, Eve and their descendants. And it begins with his covering up and clothing them.

We start to see that God's justice is never known in isolation from his love. They are both facets of God's unchanging character, his inherent glory. That character is reflected by his love and justice towards the people he has made. It's not that God is temperamental in flitting between punishment and kindness. He doesn't dish out the penalty first and then change his mind, wondering if he's been too harsh. No, it's that justice and love are inseparable and unchanging aspects of who God is.

Some people have wondered if the animal skins required for these clothes pre-empt sacrifice as the means of atoning for sin. They argue that God covers over their shame through an animal's sacrificial death. Well, it's certainly possible, but even if you don't find that persuasive, there's no doubt that here humanity begins its encounter with the grace of God.

It's also worth noting the serpent's punishment, which is the first sighting of an even more glorious grace still to come:

> I will put
>   enmity between you and the woman,
>   and between your offspring and hers;
> he will crush your head,
>   and you will strike his heel.

(Gen. 3:15)

We are told that one of Eve's offspring will eventually deal the serpent a lethal blow. More on that later.

For now, let's pause and marvel at how God responds to their sin. Yes, there is punishment, but it doesn't end the relationship between Creator and creation. The whole episode concludes with the message that God would continue to care for them. The Lord provides clothes for their immediate need, and one day will provide a serpent-slayer for their greatest need.

The glory of God's grace is that he upholds both the seriousness of sin and a commitment to love. We see that here in the Garden of Eden, and we see it again in another garden, Gethsemane. There, on the eve of his crucifixion, Jesus acknowledges the seriousness of God's justice: 'My Father, if it is possible, may this cup be taken from me' (Matt. 26:39).

The cup has long been a symbol of God's righteous anger against sin and the strength of his justice. Centuries before Jesus' prayer in the garden, the prophets Isaiah and Jeremiah used the cup as an image of God's judgment against the wickedness of his people and the surrounding nations (Is. 51:17–23; Jer. 25:15–27). Later, in John's book of Revelation, the image of the cup reappears as the punishment prepared for the evil one and those who worship him (Rev. 14:9–10).

Yet Jesus, God himself, commits to drink the cup of a punishment he did not deserve. Jesus drains the cup so that forgiveness would pour out to those who had rejected him. Justice is satisfied but the guilty who turn to Christ are set free. In other words, the cross is the most breathtaking display of grace. In Jesus' death we see this glorious union of God's justice and love. I love the way William Rees expressed it in his hymn 'Here Is Love':

Heaven's peace and perfect justice kissed a guilty world in love.[4]

God's grace in Genesis is an early glimpse of a recurring picture. It's like the view after the first stage of a mountain climb. The landscape is starting to appear over the ridges, but for now you're closer to the base than the summit. The scenery won't change, but as you climb your perspective will improve. So it is with the view we have of God's grace as we journey through the Bible. It's the same landscape but seen from an ever-improving elevation; the same grace but seen from an ever-improving vantage point.

God continues to respond to guilt with love, and through justice he brings peace. Whether the clothing for Adam and Eve points specifically to Christ's sacrifice or not, it is a powerful image of God's grace towards those who have rejected him.

GLORIOUS RESTORATION

So how can we know the glory of God's grace for ourselves? What impact does it have on life now and in eternity?

If you're anything like me, you don't need to think too hard to recognise your need for God's grace. I go after

---

[4] William Rees, 'Here Is Love Vast as the Ocean', 1855 (trans. William Edwards, 1915).

things I know are not God's design for me; I question whether God's ways are best; I act as if I'd be better off on my own terms. In other words, I regularly fall short of the glory of God. The truth is that if there is a holy God, I have no more right to a place with him than Adam, Eve or anyone else. If I believe what the Bible says about sin, I can have no expectation that God will look kindly on me.

I could expect nothing but justice, that is, until I take in this view of God's glorious grace. The first sight we have is this provision for Adam and Eve *after* their rebellion. This refrain of undeserved kindness then repeats throughout the Bible until its crescendo on the cross.

How do you imagine God looks on you?

If your view doesn't take in the reality of your sin, I would suggest that you're not really looking at all. You won't get far up a mountain with your eyes closed. But if you've got stuck on the ledge from where you can see your guilt and nothing more, then you need to look again. What is it that bursts into view in the Bible's revelation of God? Grace: undeserved and limitless love towards fallen people like you and me. And, at the centre of God's grace, is restoration of our relationship with him. This is a relationship that we were created to enjoy, and that gives us life.

This extraordinary grace is not just good for us as sinners; it is an aspect of God's glory that will be praised throughout eternity. Paul writes that what God has done for us in Christ is 'to the praise of his glorious grace' (Eph. 1:6). No angel will sing as passionately as those who've experienced this grace for themselves. This will be our anthem as we sing about the wonder of his love.

And we can have more than just a glimpse of this grace. Receiving God's forgiveness means more than looking forward to heaven. When we ask for God's forgiveness, we receive it as a life-changing gift. Ponder what it means to live understanding that God, who knows everything about you, loves you. Anything that you think might bring you shame and condemnation has been covered over by Jesus' sacrificial blood. He died in your place so that you would be with him forever.

Through faith in him, you and I are brought inside this same glorious story. We're shown the same grace and restored with the same love. It's his grace that saves us and which fuels our transformation. If you're reading this and you've never known that grace, it's never too soon to turn to Jesus and receive it.

When we see this, it really is breathtaking. We can live in the freedom of unconditional love. Rather than desperately trying to earn God's favour and being fearful that we could fall out of his care, we're given assurance that nothing can separate us from his love.

That's not a freedom to continue in rebellion. Our awareness of God's love will help us live to please him. First, we turn and acknowledge our sin. Then, having received his grace, we can live in the power of his Holy Spirit. We discover the joy and fulfilment of living for the one who loves us like that.

But God's grace is a sight we need to constantly recall. It is not only for that initial moment of restoration. We need to keep returning to the view of God's grace and his power to change us. As we live in the light of God's glorious grace, he replaces our false desires with godly desires that bring a fullness of life with him.

TAKE IN THE VIEW

In this chapter, we began with the sin of Adam and Eve. It was a terrible insult to the God who made them and walked with them in the garden. In contrast to their inglorious rebellion, we saw God's opening act of grace. He clothed and cared for them, despite what they had done. Even the punishments concerning childbearing and death would be the means of God's grace entering the human story. Jesus, God born into humanity, would die to bring us life. The descendant of Adam and Eve would put an end to the curse of sin.

It's the first glimpse we see of God's gracious character. It's an early view of his mercy, even towards those who have rejected him. God embarks on a relentless pursuit of a lost people, to bring us back to the joy of knowing him. And this commitment to gracious love will be a song of praise that the redeemed will sing for eternity.

We begin that song now, as we make our way along life's journey. So, as we climb, remind yourself of the one we're heading towards and let his glory inspire you along the way.

Before we move on, why not take a moment to savour that view of his love?

Perhaps pray and thank the Lord for his grace towards you.

3

STAR-FILLED SKIES IN AN OLD MAN'S EYES

THE GLORY OF GOD'S FAITHFULNESS

He took him outside and said, 'Look up at the sky and count the stars – if indeed you can count them.' Then he said to him, 'So shall your offspring be.'

(Gen. 15:5)

Despite God's grace towards Adam and Eve, the human story deteriorates from bad to worse. One generation after the serpent and the fruit, a pattern of sin has developed. Driven by envy, Cain murders his brother Abel.

By Genesis 6, rebellion has spread so far that only Noah's family are saved from the flood, and only then by God's favour. By Genesis 11, the people of Babel, puffed up with pride, try to build their way to heaven. It is a desperate pursuit of self-glory, as they shamelessly declare their aim to 'make a name for ourselves' (Gen. 11:4).

The futility of that plan is made clear when God has to peer down to see their efforts. The account is almost sarcastic in its dismissal of human arrogance. And that means that at the end of Genesis 11, we're left with a rather forlorn cliffhanger: where does humanity go from here?'

We've seen God's glory in his grace, but will we ever move on? Does grace simply create an infinite loop of human sin and divine forgiveness?

The answer is a common one in Scripture: God takes the initiative. He launches his plan to break the cycle. He directs a man called Abram to leave his home in Ur and lead his family towards a new land. Along the way, God promises Abram and his wife Sarai that they will have a son.

It must be one of the most audacious statements ever made. Here is an elderly man, married to an elderly lady, and they have been unable to have children. Then, one evening, God leads him out of his tent under a clear night sky.

The first time I experienced a truly clear night was on a visit to Guinea in West Africa. Earlier in the day, we'd driven out of the city to help at a youth camp. That evening, Joseph, our driver, and I were outside, trying to teach each other some songs. I wouldn't like to comment on the performance, but on a clear night, miles from any sources of light, the backdrop for our impromptu concert was illuminated by thousands and thousands of pinpricks of light. I saw, for the first time, how the stars really can fill the sky.

NASA currently estimates that there are at least one hundred billion stars in our galaxy. They're not all visible from earth, but enough are that the effect would have been dramatic when God said to Abram, 'count the stars – if indeed you can' (Gen. 15:5).

That seems tough on a man whose eyesight is probably not what it once was. But God isn't testing him; he is making an extraordinary promise. God has already told them they would have offspring to fill the land. That was incredible enough. Now the scale of that promise expands to include descendants as numerous as the grains of dust on earth (Gen. 13:16) and the stars in the sky. It's hard to overstate how unlikely that must have seemed. Abram had been on his knees before God as his hopes of an heir faded. He could only imagine that his inheritance would pass to someone other than his own child. He had even cried out to the Lord, 'You have given me no children; so a servant in my household will be my heir' (Gen. 15:3).

We all know what it's like when people don't keep their word. Even promises made with good intentions will sometimes be broken. It can be an extremely painful experience, especially when the promise is significant. Perhaps Abram felt like that – maybe even more so, since it was a promise made by the God he'd followed to a foreign land. If God's promise wasn't kept, Abram's journey would all have been for nothing.

PROMISES MADE

If God only made little promises, the fact he kept them could hardly be called glorious. But the God of the Bible makes big promises. Really big. Imagine you're the one under a star-filled sky and start counting. You're well past an age you could have children, and you're long past trying. Then God speaks and promises that your offspring will outnumber those stars. How would you feel?

Of course, anyone can make big promises. It's keeping them that's difficult. Think how different life would be if we kept every promise and stuck to every word. Sadly, it's an impossible dream. Situations change, commitments fade and none of us is perfect. I make small promises and I still struggle to keep them. I've lost count of the times I've said I'll take the bin out, only to realise it's mysteriously made its own way outside a day later. But God makes big promises and keeps them. The glorious faithfulness of God is revealed as he sticks to his Word – every single time.

Still, there are plenty of twists and turns along the way, mostly due to God's people wandering off track. Sometime later, when Abram still has no children, Sarai convinces Abram to take matters into his own hands. They find it too tempting to reduce God's promise to something more feasible. Like the serpent in the garden, you can almost hear them ask, 'Did God *really* say?' So, instead of trusting God, they look to conceive a son through Hagar, Sarai's servant. The glory of God's promise is reduced to the suggestion that 'perhaps I can build a family through her' (Gen. 16:2). Abram acquiesces and Hagar, well, she is given no choice. Ishmael is born, but he is not the son of the promise. It's a sad chapter in the life of someone often named a 'hero' of the faith.

Yet, once again, the glory of God shines even more brightly against this backdrop of human failure. The Lord knew that this would happen. He knew that Abram and Sarai would find it too hard to believe the promise. Yet he still made and kept his Word.

In fact, the Lord gives Abram a sign that this promise will rest solely on God's own faithfulness. After Abram looks to the stars, he falls into a deep sleep. A great darkness comes over him as a sign that God is on the move.

If you've ever read through the Bible, you may have noticed some of the seemingly unusual ways in which agreements were sealed in the different cultures. Take the end of Ruth's story, for example, when Boaz redeems her by taking off a sandal (Ruth 4:8).

Now, if you think that sounds strange, listen to the way God confirms his agreement with Abram. Abram is told to sacrifice several animals and separate the butchered pieces into two lines. Normally (that is, as normal as lines of animal carcasses can be), the two people entering an agreement would then both walk between the lines. Instead, only God (represented by a smoking fire-pot) passes between them.

Some people have seen this as God offering his own sacrificial death as part of the agreement. Perhaps God is saying, 'Even if you break the promise, I will pay the price.' That would fit with the unfolding drama of redemption. After generations of Abraham's descendants continue to turn away, God comes to be the sacrifice. But even if that interpretation stretches the symbolism too far, we know that God alone passes through the lines that night. God alone will be faithful to the promise. It will be God who keeps his Word.

And so he does. By the time we reach Genesis 21, Abram and Sarai have painted the spare room and hung a mobile over the cot. Isaac, their son, is born. God also gives them new names. Now called Abraham and Sarah, they will be the parents of a multitude of people.

Thankfully for Abraham and Sarah (and us), God's promises are not dependent on the faithfulness of the beneficiary. God's Word is gloriously dependent on *his* faithfulness. That is a wonderful thing to know. God promises blessings to people who don't deserve them, and who don't even believe they'll come true. If that's you, be reassured that you're in good company.

We see the glory of God not only when he makes extraordinary promises, but when he keeps them. As Psalm 115:1 puts it, 'Not to us, LORD, not to us but to your name be the glory, because of your love and *faithfulness*' (my italics).

And not only does God remain faithful, but he is faithful to people like Abraham and Sarah. People who don't deserve God's blessing are promised it anyway.

Perhaps you sometimes wonder if you really can trust the Lord to work all things for the good of those who love him? If so, look at Abraham and believe that God is faithful and trustworthy.

PROMISES FULFILLED

At the same time, we must be careful how we apply God's promises. There are some verses in the Bible, particularly God's promises, which make great posts on social media. They sound lovely – who doesn't want to be told that the Lord has 'plans to prosper you and not to harm you'? (Jer. 29:11) But these promises can be damaging when they're lifted out of their context. We risk a great disappointment when things don't turn out as God has apparently promised. Just because God told Abraham he would have a son, that doesn't mean we can promise pregnancy to a couple praying through childlessness. Similarly, even though God promised the Israelites a hope and a future after Babylon, we mustn't promise the earthly health and wealth of a false gospel.

Instead, it is when we see these promises fulfilled for the original recipient that we are shown the faithfulness of God. It's knowing that God kept his extraordinary promise to Abraham that helps us trust the promises which do apply. We can trust the promise of his love and new life in Christ because the same God has a perfect record of keeping his Word. We don't need every promise to apply to us in order to be able to love and worship our faithful Lord.

Yet there's a way in which this ancient promise does still apply. Through one of Abraham's descendants, God continues to draw people into his family. God had already planned that this promise would extend to a world that Abraham didn't know existed. I mean, Abraham didn't believe that he would have a son, let alone grandchildren and a nation. How would he have coped with the idea that his family would eventually include millions, probably billions, of people?

Have you seen those star-naming gifts? For a fee (of course) you can receive a pack which allows you to register someone's name for a star. I'm not sure what you do afterwards, or who's decided they have the right to name stars. Besides, God saw fit to create one hundred billion stars in each of the one hundred billion or more galaxies, so good luck spotting the one you named after your Granny. But you don't need to pay for the privilege anyway. The one who brought those stars into existence had a further promise up his sleeve. From before time began, God had you in mind as a future member of Abraham's family. So when he pointed Abraham to the sky that night, one of those stars already represented you.

The way God keeps his promise of a family for Abraham is initially biological. The fulfilment begins through Isaac, then Jacob and his twelve sons. It progresses as that family, despite many setbacks, grows into the people of Israel. There are ways to become Jewish, but for the most part membership comes through birth. Then, after hundreds of years, that family comes to include a baby boy born in

Bethlehem. In Jesus, this promise to Abraham reaches its glorious fulfilment. Jesus' death and resurrection removes the division between Abraham's family and those outside it. In Christ, God is creating one new people from Jews and Gentiles. Through faith in Jesus, we can now become children of Abraham.

The book of Acts describes the spread of that message going out from Jerusalem in the months and years after Jesus' resurrection. No one is more influential in the spread of that message than the apostle Paul, but he hadn't always seen it that way.

Paul had always been an ardent believer in God's promise to Abraham. But earlier in his life he hated the idea that belonging to God's family would now come through faith in Jesus. Everything changed when he met the risen Lord on the road to Damascus. He realised that Abraham's descendants included those who recognise Jesus as the fulfilment of God's promises. Later, he confirmed that new faith when he wrote to the church in Galatia, 'Understand, then, that those who have faith are children of Abraham' (Gal. 3:7). Paul came to see that the family tree has far more branches than he'd imagined.

So if you're someone who has faith in Jesus, God had already planned to bring you inside that family. When Abraham looked up that night, there was already a star with your name on it. You know this promise came true because you're part of the fulfilment. If you're in Christ, then you are one of the descendants illuminating Abraham's sky.

TAKE IN THE VIEW

This may be another good moment to slow down and take in the view. If you want to push the mountain-climb metaphor, it's time to open the thermos and dig out the Kendal mint cake.

How often do you see yourself as an answer to a 4,000-year-old promise?

Do you know that the God who kept this promise will promise eternal life to you too?

What a difference it makes when we know that God's Word is trustworthy. And the best way to discover this is by putting that trust into action.

I've always been intrigued by the idea of skydiving. To date my only foray into the world of adrenaline sport was a spot of mild abseiling as a teenager. But I can see that there is a thrill to jumping out of a plane at 15,000 feet. However, if I were to go up to skydive, would I have the guts to go through with it? Would I really trust that parachute to work as planned? I imagine I could hear all the safety talks, watch them packing the main chute and the back-up into the bag, but even then have doubts. If I was stood there with the door open and the sound of the wind rushing past the plane, would I trust enough to jump? I guess there's only one way I'll ever find out. We only ever really know if we can trust something or someone when we take the plunge – or, as in my parachuting example, when we literally step out in faith.

Maybe it can feel like that sometimes when we're called to trust God. It's only when we begin to step out in faith that we discover his Word is secure and he will not let us fall. But we can have confidence to take that step because we've seen the glory of his faithfulness.

Next time you're outside on a starry night, look up at the same image of God's glory that was revealed to Abraham. Yes, there's a revelation of God's glory in the vastness of space. But there is also a personal revelation: God has brought you inside the promise. You can trust him.

Picturing God's faithfulness is a prompt to trust his Word and live according to the instruction of a trustworthy Lord. We can help ourselves by filling our minds with this image of the stars and so discover the joy of trusting God. If you're in Christ, then you *are* adopted into his family. You are living proof that God's promises are extravagantly made and beautifully fulfilled.

The writers of the psalms often reminded themselves of God's faithfulness, especially when their faith was tested. Maybe these verses, and this recurring theme of faithfulness which I've highlighted, will help you share their wonder at our promise-keeping God:

Teach me your way, LORD,
*   that I may rely on your faithfulness;*
give me an undivided heart,
*   that I may fear your name.*

(Ps. 86:11)

But you, LORD, are a compassionate and gracious God,
*   slow to anger, abounding in love and faithfulness.*

(Ps. 86:15)

Righteousness and justice are the foundation
of your throne;
*   love and faithfulness go before you.*

(Ps. 89:14)

He will cover you with his feathers,
and under his wings you will find refuge;
his faithfulness will be your shield and rampart.

(Ps. 91:4)

4

THUNDERING HOOVES AND AN EMPTY TOMB

THE GLORY OF GOD'S VICTORY

Then the LORD *opened the servant's eyes, and he looked and saw the hills full of horses and chariots of fire.*

(2 Kgs. 6:17)

If you're seeking glory, winning something is usually a good avenue to pursue. Of course, the glory you achieve depends on what your victory is in. I doubt there's much international acclaim for those who triumph in their family's Christmas board game. Although, judging by how seriously some of us take it, I might be wrong.

In the past, success in battle was often the sure-fire route to glory. Monarchs and emperors often turned to military conquest as a route to power and prestige. In the days of the Roman Empire, victorious generals would re-enter Rome in a huge procession, dressed in purple and gold, with the spoils of war displayed in their wake. This 'triumph' often lasted three or four days as the fame and renown of the victor was broadcast from the colonnades.

These days, the most widely praised victories often come from the world of sport. When a football team wins the Premier League, they'll often parade the trophy on open-top buses as fans line the street to celebrate. When London hosted the Olympics in 2012, Royal Mail repainted the letterboxes gold in the hometowns of victorious athletes. There was something wonderfully British in combining international sporting triumph with the routine function of posting a letter.

I've come to learn that my hopes for sporting glory will never be matched by my ability to win. Having said that, my friend and I did win our college's table-football tournament. In fact, I was prepared to study for as many years as necessary to get my name on that illustrious trophy. In the end, after too many hours on the table, we triumphed. Unfortunately, the adulation from (both) the spectators was limited by the amount they knew we'd practised. There wasn't much glory in defeating opponents who'd had better things to do in the weeks (and months) we'd spent fine-tuning our skills.

We tend to find greater glory in those who triumph against the odds, or when success is snatched from the jaws of defeat. Everyone loves a good comeback – claiming victory just as it seems that all hope is lost.

As you read through the Bible, there are times when it seems as if hope is lost. There are moments when it looks like evil will win the day. These periods sometimes include a long wait before anything like a glorious victory or restoration comes about. If we didn't know the whole story, it could seem that God was either unwilling or unable to bring his people through their (usually self-inflicted) hardship.

Abraham's offspring spent four hundred years in Egypt, mostly as slaves, before their exodus. Then they experience forty years wandering in the desert due to their lack of faith, and more than sixty years in Babylon, before God uses a foreign king to send them home. Even so, as the final Old Testament prophet anticipates the coming Saviour, there are still four hundred years or so to wait.

We shouldn't skip over these pauses in God's salvation story; his timing is not like ours. His plan for a glorious victory can involve a significant wait whilst history holds its breath. That means his people often go through a period of refining as they look for his salvation.

Yet, behind the scenes, God is working his purposes out. Even when it looks like events are out of control, we discover that God is planning it for good. One of my favourite examples, and one of the most memorable, happens during the time of Israel's kings.

By this time, the descendants of Abraham are a nation. They live in the land promised to their forefather, but it is not a rediscovery of paradise. Under 'judges', called by God to lead his people, they have continued to do what is right in their own eyes. After they plead with God to be like the neighbouring nations, he then appoints kings over them – Saul, David, Solomon and so on. Even then their faithfulness to God continues to ebb and flow. Throughout this whole period, it is often the prophets who call the people back to God. By 2 Kings 6, the foremost prophet in Israel is Elisha, but it looks as though he is about to suffer a terrible defeat.

PROTECTED

As we join the story, the situation for Elisha and those with him appears hopeless. Elisha is under threat because he has been rescuing God's people from the Arameans with miraculous insight into their battle plans. Frustrated by this unusual disadvantage, the Arameans therefore dispatch their forces to seize Elisha. They track him and his servant to the city of Dothan and surround it, ready to take them by force, perhaps even to kill them.

In the morning, Elisha's servant ventures outside and sees a vast opposing army. With their enemies surrounding them, he asks what seems like a reasonable question: 'Oh no, my lord! What shall we do?' (2 Kgs. 6:15). They are completely outnumbered, and victory seems to be heading to the enemies of God's people. However, Elisha has learned to trust the Lord and he gives an extraordinary reply: 'Don't be afraid ... Those who are with us are more than those who are with them' (2 Kgs. 6:16).

What must that young man have thought at this? He knows there are only a few of them but hundreds, perhaps thousands, of professional soldiers who are heavily armed and ready to charge. Perhaps he thinks their impending defeat has sent his master over the edge! How could there be more of them? If ever there was a time to panic, surely this was it. But God is about to reveal the glory of his hidden victory; the outward appearance is not always the deeper reality.

What happens next is amazing. Elisha prays, 'Open his eyes, LORD, so that he may see' (2 Kgs. 6:17). The young man looks again, and this time he sees the mountain full of heaven's horses and chariots of fire. We're not given much detail about those heavenly armies. We're not told if he could hear the sounds of their hooves, or whether their wheels threw up dust from the ground. We're invited to picture for ourselves what that must have been like. What we do know is that they fill the mountain and form a protective barrier around Elisha and his servant. What an image of divine security; God will win the day.

It's easy to sympathise with Elisha's servant when he first looked out. They were hemmed in, outnumbered and in real danger for their lives. Yet this account typifies a recurring theme of the Bible: God will win the victory for good, but it is often initially unseen. This young man was given a glimpse behind the scenes. Yes, they were surrounded, but by the horses and chariots of an unseen heavenly army. It was a vision of the glory of God's victory.

In the end, Elisha insists that the Arameans are spared. Instead, they are temporarily blinded and taken to the Israelite king. Once there, their sight is restored, they are given a feast and then released. Elisha has such confidence in God's victory that there is no need to respond with violence. Instead, he seeks a transformation of the whole conflict.

I love the horses and chariots of fire coming into view just as hope seems lost. It's a picture to keep in mind when you can't see how God's purposes will prevail. As humans we're often quick to assume that reality is limited to what we can see or measure. But because Elisha sees the glorious protection of God, he can trust. More than that, he is so assured of victory that he doesn't seek the enemy's destruction. Instead, trusting God's victory, he can feed them and return them home.

TRIUMPHANT

It's worth noting that most of us are in a very different situation than Elisha today (although many believers are still suffering and even dying for their faith). But during the time of Israel's kings, the enemies of God's people tended to ride horses and chariots. So the Lord used military victories to safeguard his people until the Messiah was born. Yet the final victory was never going to be over human armies. The glory of God's triumph was never going to come through the sword.

Jesus announces a new and decisive means of conquering evil on the eve of his crucifixion. He does so in the Garden of Gethsemane, as the soldiers arrive to arrest him. Peter, always one for action, draws his sword and cuts off a soldier's ear. But Jesus steps forward, heals the soldier and says to Peter, 'Put your sword away! Shall I not drink the cup the Father has given me?' (John 18:11). Jesus knows that the battle for God's victory over evil is entering a new phase, and he is about to unleash the lethal blow: his death and resurrection.

A few years later, Paul writes along similar lines to the believers in Ephesus, pointing out that, 'our struggle is not against flesh and blood' (Eph. 6:12). Instead, the final victory is over the evil that sin brought into creation, and over Satan the chief protagonist.

In chapter two, we saw a glimpse of God's grace that brought forgiveness to sinful humanity. That grace comes to us through Jesus' death and resurrection. But the cross and empty tomb are also the decisive moment of God's glorious triumph over evil. And yet, like the unseen army surrounding Elisha and his servant, that victory is not immediately visible. I imagine the forces of evil must have been pinching themselves when Jesus died, exclaiming, 'Is this the Son of God hung up on a criminal's cross?' For a few dark hours, they may even have believed that God's plan had been defeated.

However, Jesus had already explained that his death and resurrection are the heart of God's victory. His death is, in fact, the climax of God's plan.

On the eve of his crucifixion, Jesus gathers his disciples together. During the evening, he prays, 'Father, the hour has come. Glorify your Son, that your Son may glorify you' (John 17:1). Jesus knows that he will achieve a final victory over evil and, in doing so, bring glory to the Father. In fact, the focus on glory in Jesus' prayer is unrelenting. He continues, 'I have brought you *glory* on earth by finishing the work you gave me to do. And now, Father, *glorify* me in your presence with the *glory* I had with you before the world began' (John 17:4–5, my italics). As unlikely as it appears, the cross also reveals Jesus' glory. His death and resurrection are the moment of his victory.

Even though Jesus has explained this to his disciples, they desert him. It appears as if the worst has happened – that evil has won, and God was powerless to prevent it. On the surface, and especially to a Jew, death on a cross is about as *in*glorious as it gets. But, as with Elisha's servant, the deeper truth soon becomes visible. Later, when the risen Jesus opens their eyes, the disciples see that the cross and empty tomb are, in fact, his glorious triumph.

Paul writes to the Colossians, '[Jesus] disarmed the powers and authorities, he made a public spectacle of them, triumphing over them by the cross' (Col. 2:15). Yet at the time, that glorious triumph was not apparent. It seemed that Jesus was the public spectacle. Like the chariots of fire, the victory was initially hidden.

So how can we have the eyes of faith to see God's victory?

I would love to see chariots of fire around me when I head into difficult situations. I could imagine a few occasions when a heavenly army would be rather persuasive. You certainly wouldn't get cut up on the motorway if your car came with an optional extra of flaming chariots. But we have something far better – the resurrected Jesus and the presence of his Spirit.

This is an occasion when a vivid and biblical imagination can make a huge difference to the challenges we might face. Can you picture Jesus' tomb on the first Easter morning? It doesn't matter too much whether your image is historically accurate as long as you've got the important detail: it's empty.

As surely as the tomb was empty that morning, so sure is God's conquest of evil, sin and death. As definitively as he triumphed over the grave, so definitively does he promise to overcome opposition to his people. We have more than the presence of chariots of fire; we live in the presence of God and the assurance of his victory.

It's easy to worry for our situations as Elisha's servant did. But the eyes of faith reveal God's victory, won for his glory by Jesus. Because of all that he's done, we can trust that God's goodness will triumph. That is gloriously good news.

TRANSFORMED

There are, however, questions that remain. If Jesus has won a glorious victory, why is there still so much suffering in the world? Shouldn't Christ's triumph mean we live free from the effects of evil?

Some preachers will try and tell you exactly that. They'll say that the only cause of unhealed illness or problems in life is a lack of faith. I can't help feeling their message would be more convincing if they shared their platform with 200-year-old Christians who'd 'had the faith to never get sick'. The thing is that these preachers have missed the point. The Bible does describe miracles and answers to prayer that continue after Christ's resurrection, but they are not guaranteed in this life. It would be cruel of God to keep us in this world forever whilst a defeated evil digs in its dying claws. No, the victory Christ has won will be complete when he returns and brings his eternal kingdom. The promise of a final victory over sickness and death is in the new creation.

Yes, Jesus' victory over sin can and will have an impact in this life. The more our hearts love with Christ-like conviction, the more we will bring a radical, sacrificial love to the people we meet. The greater we treasure Christ, the easier it will be to reject the false idols of material wealth and exploitation of the earth. In that sense, there are victories to be won that are very visible. But just like Elisha's army and Jesus' cross, the biggest victory is often unseen. It is hearts set free from the tyranny of sin and reset on a path to glory.

There is an unseen victory that is ours in Christ: the promise that even death has lost its sting. The only thing that can separate us from God's presence is our sin, but when we hand that to Jesus, it is nailed to his cross. Paul is adamant that there is nothing that can now separate believers from the love of God – in this life, and in eternity. Jesus' victory means nothing can stand in his way of bringing a redeemed people to share in his glory.

When I was younger and fitter, I took part in the Three Peaks Challenge to climb the highest mountains in Scotland, England and Wales within twenty-four hours. We began at Ben Nevis at 4 a.m. and, being somewhat competitive, were keen to get up and down as quickly as possible. However, near the top we came across a large sheet of ice. Crossing on foot appeared treacherous and would mean very slow progress. It was hard to see how best to proceed. That was until one of the more inventive members of our group sat down and simply slid himself across. Sometimes the way past life's challenges is not immediately apparent. Sometimes the path God calls us on appears impassable. But he has already made it across and he will see his people through. Even death has been overcome in Christ's victory. I try and remember that by adding a two-word subtitle when I picture his empty tomb: 'Jesus wins'.

TAKE IN THE VIEW

As you pause and picture God's fiery chariots and Jesus' empty tomb, what do these victories mean for life in a good but fallen world?

First, we know that there is power over evil in the name of Jesus. We can work for real change in this world because Jesus has triumphed and the final victory is certain. That must be an inspiration to live courageously for the Lord, knowing that God will even use our death to bring us to glory. It's true freedom to take a stand for good, because the outcome is assured and our hope is secure.

Secondly, we can live in the knowledge that nothing can separate us from God's love. We can live with a humble confidence that the world does not provide, knowing that God works for the good of those who love him. He has won a glorious victory.

Are you facing a situation that appears hopeless? I don't want to pretend that the answer is easy, but we can trust that whatever lies ahead, it cannot keep us from our Lord and Saviour.

The best thing to do is be honest with God when we feel hopeless.

Ask for a reminder of his unseen victory.

5

THE LION IS THE LAMB

THE GLORY OF GOD IN CHRIST

Then I saw a Lamb, looking as if it had been slain,
standing at the centre of the throne.

(Rev. 5:6)

In my final year at secondary school, a group of us went mountaineering in Wales. My highlight was the night we camped on a mountain in Snowdonia. We climbed to the ridge where we would sleep, ready to head to the summit in the morning. As we went up, we could only see a short way in front because of the swirling mist. But by the morning, the clouds had lifted. As we emerged from our tents, we were greeted with a breathtaking sight over the mountains towards a winding strip of coastline. It was the widest open space I had ever seen, as the jagged ridges of the mountain range straightened out towards the sea. And we knew that the view would only improve as we continued to the peak.

Revelation is the final book in the Bible, and the final word on God's glory before Christ returns. It's the penultimate ridge on the mountain climb; the closest thing we have to the view we will one day enjoy in full. It's as if we start to climb above the clouds and take in the clearest sight of God's glory this side of eternity.

WORTHY IS THE LAMB

The book of Revelation is a series of visions that were given to the apostle John during his exile on the island of Patmos. The first three chapters contain letters from Jesus to seven contrasting churches, urging them to be faithful. They are often the subject of sermons, and rightly so as they remain highly relevant. Sadly, the number of sermon series that continue beyond Revelation 3 is probably much smaller. But the motivation to live this radical faith is surely the vision of God's glory which is unfolded through the rest of John's book.

Revelation 4 begins to reveal an image of God in the splendour of heaven. You can almost hear John struggling for words to describe the scene. As he is led in, he sees a throne. On the throne is one with the appearance of jasper and ruby, encircled by an emerald rainbow. Around the throne are twenty-four elders, dressed in white and wearing crowns of gold. There are flashes of lightning and thunder, then John also sees burning lamps and a sea of glass as clear as crystal. Within the throne room are four living creatures, covered in eyes and made up of great and mighty beasts. Together with the elders they sing, 'You are worthy, our Lord and God, to receive glory and honour and power' (Rev. 4:11). These creatures are more impressive than anything you or I have ever seen. Yet even they cannot help but fall before God and acknowledge his all-surpassing glory. John has been given, quite simply, the clearest view of God's glory that any human has been privileged to see.

But somehow there's more to come. Revelation 5 pulls together the glimpses of glory that have been appearing since Genesis. And, in doing so, it elevates our perspective on God's glory to an even higher level.

In the vision, John is made aware of a significant scroll. It's written on both sides, symbolising a vast quantity of writing. It's sealed with seven seals, to indicate that only a perfect individual will be able to break them and discover what is written. This scroll represents the final actions of history as God redeems and restores his creation. When the scroll is opened, the glorious victory and eternal reign of God's kingdom will come.

But a question rings out from a 'mighty' angel: 'Who is worthy to break the seals and open the scroll?' (Rev. 5:2). The four incredible creatures are not worthy, nor are the elders. Not even this strong angel is worthy to break those seals. Unless someone is found, the scroll will remain closed and God's plan will remain unfulfilled. John even begins to cry because no one seems worthy of the honour to open it. He longs for God's plan to come to fruition. He knows the persecution God's people are enduring at the same time he is receiving this vision. He is desperate for that final judgment to come and vindicate those who are in Christ. No wonder he weeps.

So, for a terrifying moment, it seems as if no one is deserving of the glory to open this scroll. But then one of the elders says to John, 'Do not weep! See, the Lion of the tribe of Judah, the Root of David, has triumphed. He is able to open the scroll and its seven seals' (Rev. 5:5).

John turns to look. Presumably he is expecting to see a great lion – a creature more powerful and impressive than those he's already seen. A lion would certainly seem to fit the bill – the king of the animals, noble and majestic. Instead, in the centre of the emerald rainbow, the elders with their golden crowns and incredible beasts … the Lion is a Lamb: 'a Lamb, looking as if it had been slain, standing at the centre of the throne' (Rev. 5:6).

At the very centre of God's glorious throne room is a Lamb, and one that still bears the scars of sacrifice. A Lamb that was dead now stands in glory.

This is Jesus, bearing the marks of his crucifixion. In him, the earlier glimpses of God's glory are drawn together into the most glorious image of all. Here is a foretaste of what we will see and enjoy forever. He is the Lion of Judah, the Lamb who was slain. And as he takes the scroll, the creatures and the elders sing a new song:

You are worthy to take the scroll
and to open its seals,
because you were slain,
and with your blood you purchased for God
persons from every tribe and language and people
and nation.
You have made them to be a kingdom and priests to
serve our God,
and they will reign on the earth.

(Rev. 5:9–10)

This Lamb has fulfilled God's plan of redemption. He is worthy to break the seals and deliver the final act. That is why these heavenly creatures sing with such adoration. The glory they attribute to the Lamb is almost indescribable.

Then, incredibly, the glory is ratcheted up. Myriads and myriads and thousands of thousands of angels sing out,

Worthy is the Lamb, who was slain,
to receive power and wealth and wisdom and strength
and honour and glory and praise!

(Rev. 5:12)

If you've ever sung in a large congregation, you'll know how moving it can be as voices rise together in harmony. Imagine how this heavenly choir must sound. And yet even this is not the end of the glory that is given to this

Lamb. We've seen elders, creatures and innumerable angels praising the Lamb, but,

> Then I heard every creature in heaven and on earth and under the earth and in the sea, and all that is in them, saying,
>
> 'To him who sits on the throne and to the Lamb
> be praise and honour and glory and power,
> for ever and ever!'
>
> (Rev. 5:13)

John sees *everything* giving glory to the Lamb. Alongside God the Father, Jesus the Son is worthy of unending worship and praise. If you're trusting in him, you will experience this glory in person. You will be there in the multitude, singing his praise.

Growing up, I enjoyed the occasional computer game, and especially the simulations of racing cars and football. Back then the computers were far less powerful, so they concentrated the graphics on the main action, and the crowd was a sort of indistinct blob. These days, though, even the crowds in computer games have realistic features; you can see their individual faces.

I used to visualise this passage like the old computer games, with no detail in the crowd of worshippers. But unlike those games, God's vision has no limitations, so he could have shown John the real faces of the multitude who will worship the Lamb. That means John might have seen your face in the crowd. Just think about that for a moment. As John took in this preview of Christ's eternal glory, he may have seen you there. Standing around you would have been family and friends – past, present and future. One day this won't just be John's prophecy; it will be your reality. You will know the joy of fulfilling all that you were made for, sharing in the glory of the Lord.

THE GLORY OF THE LAMB

As we've taken in some views of God's glory in the previous chapters, I've focussed on the revelation of God's grace, faithfulness and victory. That's because in this hymn of praise we find those same aspects of God's glory, praised in eternity.

They sing that the Lamb is worthy because his scars proclaim his glorious grace. This Lamb is a substitute, whose blood has ransomed a people for God. Their praise invites us to look at the depth of his love and to remember his sacrifice. See the mercy of God who died in the place of sinners, that those sinners might have life. By his blood he has redeemed us out of sin and death. This is *the glory of God's grace.*

The Lamb is also worthy because, through him, God's glorious promises are fulfilled. The promise to Abraham was descendants as numerous as the stars. The redeemed praising the Lamb are from every tribe, language, people and nation. In other words, we hear a global choir as numerous as the stars in Abraham's sky. This is *the glory of God's faithfulness.*

Finally, the Lamb is worthy because those people will share in the rule of his glorious kingdom. This is not militaristic imperialism. Creation is restored through loving sacrifice and will flourish under the liberating rule of its Creator. God's people will serve as priests and reign with him. Jesus' victory inaugurates a kingdom free from death, mourning, crying and pain. This is *the glory of God's victory.*

When we were young, my brother and I had a poster in our bedroom of a kingfisher. It was sat on a 'No Fishing' sign with a fish in its mouth. It was there to remind us that when we said sorry to God, we weren't to go fishing. By this I mean that when we confess our sin, it's gone, and we shouldn't go trawling it back up. That was a helpful picture of God's forgiveness for two young boys. But whilst the results of sin have been removed once for all from us, the marks of the cross are still visible on the Lamb. However, Jesus' wounds are not there for our shame; they are there as a testimony to his glorious grace, faithfulness and victory.

Under the previous Old Testament system of temples, priests and sacrifices, people would bring animals, including lambs, to be offered at the altar. The priests and their assistants would receive them and check for blemishes and defects. The animals were held up that they might be seen to be spotless. Now, at the climax of history, the one who lived a spotless life is held up that creation might see his scars. Those marks tell the story of Christ dying for our sin, creating a new people and winning a victory over death. Glory to the Lamb who was slain!

BEHOLD THE LAMB

As we've taken in those earlier glimpses of God's glory, we've paused to consider what they mean for us here and now:

- The view of God's grace prompts repentance and a desire to sin no more.

- The view of God's faithfulness strengthens trust in the Lord and his Word.

- The view of God's victory inspires belief that God's goodness will triumph.

So what can we take from this view of God's glory – the Lion and the Lamb?

I'm not sure there is anything to do other than to worship him. In translating Revelation, the English Standard Version follows the King James Version in using the word 'behold' for John's imperative to 'look' or 'see'. It may sound a little old-fashioned, but it is a helpful instruction: *behold* Jesus in his glory. We're near to the summit of the mountain now. We can have a final pause, a breather and a chance to see how close we are. Often people fall silent in those moments as they catch their breath and look out to the horizon. I doubt the word 'behold' would come into anyone's mind these days, but that's what's happening. You're so close and you've seen so much that you don't need anyone to tell you to keep going. The view itself is enough to inspire the final push.

This is an invitation to look at Jesus and see his glory. Take in the sight and allow your imagination to paint it in your mind. Then allow that reality to transform how you see everything else. All you could ever need, all the goodness you were made to worship, is found in the Lamb who died for you. The Lamb who reigns will one day bring the whole of creation to its glorious fulfilment.

I'm convinced that when we take in these sights of God's glory in Christ, we will live with ever-increasing joy and expectation. The Bible should never be reduced to a self-help guide of how to live a better life. Yes, there is wisdom for how to live faithfully and instruction for how to obey the Lord. But the desire to do so comes from awe and appreciation of who God is. He is revealed to us in the story of his gracious, faithful and victorious glory.

That is the story of redemption which Christians rehearse and proclaim as we meet in anticipation of Jesus' return. I know, for many of us, our experience of church may seem an eternity away from the sights of Revelation. But what our worship should do is call us to fix our eyes on the Lamb who was slain. We join together to retell the story of grace, faithfulness and victory in Christ. At times, we may feel small, ineffective and less-than-glorious. So here is the good news: our hope is in him. He is the Lion and the Lamb; Jesus is the glory of God. He is the one whose Spirit goes with us; he is the one whose glory we will enjoy forever. We glory in him now as we proclaim him to the world and live in the light of his victory.

TAKE IN THE VIEW

This is probably a good moment to put this book down, find a Bible and read Revelation 5.

As you do, allow yourself to picture the Lamb. Savour the view of God's breathtaking glory.

EPILOGUE:

MOUNTAIN RESCUE

We began this book by thinking about the view from a mountain. Scripture reaches its peak at the anticipation of our place with Christ in eternity. But it's not the story of us climbing closer to God. As fallen creatures, we could never get back to him by working our way up. If there's a figurative mountain separating us from God, then the Bible is not the story of holy people making their ascent. It's the story of God coming down – all the way down to the point of death as our sacrificial Lamb. He meets us at our worst, shows us grace, fulfils his promises and wins a final victory. It is his glorious triumph over evil, sin and death that we can now share.

Most mountain rescues head up to bring people back down. Jesus came down to bring us up. We see his glory because he came to us, to bring us back to him.

So don't sit back. Don't let the vision of future glory paralyse you in the present. When the path is rocky and life feels like a difficult climb, pause and take in the view. Allow the sights of God's grace, faithfulness and victory to inspire your trust in the Lord. And press on, knowing the joy of his presence with you and the promise of eternity sharing in his glory. Also, if you don't already, make sure you take regular opportunities to pause and catch your breath. Keep lifting your eyes to take in another view of God's breathtaking glory. Then remind yourself that if you think this is good, wait until he brings you to the top!

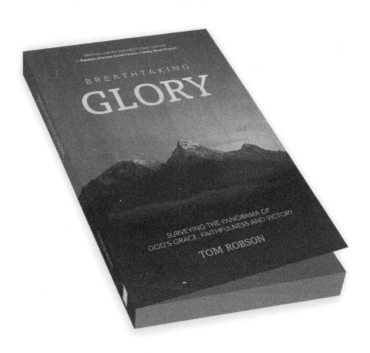

a division of **10** of those.com

10Publishing is the publishing house of **10ofThose**.
It is committed to producing quality Christian resources
that are biblical and accessible.

www.10ofthose.com is our online retail arm selling
thousands of quality books at discounted prices.

For information contact: **info@10ofthose.com**
or check out our website: **www.10ofthose.com**